THE SCARS THAT BUILT ME

Steps to Overcome Narcissist Abuse and Life Traumas

Angela Newhouse

Published by

Business Growth Advisors

SYDNEY, AUSTRALIA

You can get through it, you can survive it, and you can come out healthier and happier on the other end.

— ANGELA NEWHOUSE

Copyright © 2021 by **Angela Newhouse**

All rights reserved. No part of this publication may be reproduced, distributed or transmitted in any form or by any means, without prior written permission.

MDA Publishing
Higginbotham Rd
Gladesville, NSW, 2111
Australia

Book Layout © million-dollar author 2021

The Scars That Built Me -- 1st edition
ISBN 978-0-6450942-1-3

Introduction

Even through traumas and hardship, there is a way out. There is a bright future ahead. You can get through it, & survive it, and you can come out healthier and happier on the other end. You'll need to have faith and try to stay positive along the way.

When you survive a narcissistic relationship, one way or another, the key goals are to:

- Regain your independence mentally and physically
- Find who you are and build your life in a positive way
- Maintain physical and mental wellness

When you are in the middle of a horrible relationship, these things can seem so far away. You feel weak, you feel broken, and you feel like you are incompetent like the narcissist has made you feel for so long. You don't feel mentally well; you are stressed out the majority of the time. You have no hope that things will be better, and your health also starts to slip.

When you finally achieve these things listed above, you feel free. Freedom is having the collection of your own thoughts back and not living in fear every day. We look out in the world and see people happy and thriving, and we don't think we can get there when we are living with the trauma and all of the stress. When you get through these steps and heal yourself, it is an extraordinary sense of freedom.

Acknowledgements

Thank you to all of YOU who read this book. My dream of helping others get through the toughest of times is coming true. I want to be the light for you and be your cheerleader as you make your decision to Never Give Up and to use your Scars as steppingstones to a better life. Thank you to Martha Krejci for giving me the idea, the wisdom and the strength to find my worth and to have a voice to write this book. I couldn't have done this without you and HBR.

Thank you to my husband, my daughter, my step children and all of my friends and family who have loved me through my flaws and have been here while I healed. I may not have fallen gracefully but I have risen each time with a better view on how life should be and most importantly how it should not be. Never let the traumas of your past darken your future. I am now the person who I needed back then and I am changing lives for the better by being that person for all of you.

Always remember that the sun will shine on a new day, you always have the choice to change your circumstances and most importantly you are worthy of greatness.

The best is yet to come!

About The Author

Hi, I'm Angela.

Some people might give up after childhood traumas and live a path of destruction. Some people might give up after years of abuse from a narcissist and claim their life made them hardened and unfixable. I am not some people. I am not a victim; I am a survivor. Through multiple life traumas, years and years of very destructive abuse from a narcissist, I still refused to accept life as it was. I always knew  there was a better life out there for me, I just had to figure out how to go from broken and afraid to confident and thriving.

How was I going to do that?

- Find myself and who I really wanted to be
- Mend the broken parts
- Build the strength and knowledge to tackle any other bumps in the road that may arise

I was determined to not only survive all that was thrown my way but to show my daughter and the next generations that you must never ever give up because the sun will always come out again and the only person with the power to change your circumstances is you. With the steps laid out in the book of how I used my scars and my pain to heal and to build a better life, you can learn to thrive too. Just when I thought I was being knocked down again by health issues, I used my never give up mindset, my internal drive to be a survivor and my newly found confidence and took what I was learning about my health and developed a new business with a product that helps change lives.

With what I teach you, you can learn to stand on your own two feet, be your own advocate and have the confidence to thrive! My goal is to help 100,000 people or many more find the strength to rebuild their life after Narcissist abuse and life's traumas.

It is a very lonely, terrifying, confusing place to be and I want to help you go from broken and afraid to confident and thriving.

www.AngelaNewhouse.com
www.KureRae.com

CONTENTS

Steps to Overcome Narcissist Abuse and Life Traumas 1
Learning to Thrive 1
    The Day It Hit Me 7
BREAKING OUT 13
    Make a Plan 13
    Life After the Initial Break-Out 18
    Never Ever Give Up 25
    What is a narcissist? 27
    Isolation 32
THE STEPS TO SURVIVAL 35
    Step 1- Assessment and Planning 35
    Step 2 -Self Discovery and Learning About Your Core Values 37
    Step 3 - Health and Wellbeing is Important .. 40
    From the Outside Looking In 42
    You Are The Prey 43
    The Second-Guessing Game 45
    It's Not Just Intimate Partners 47

THE HELP YOU NEED 48
　Facts vs Feelings 48
　• I don't want this style of life anymore ... 49
　• I don't want the danger factor in my life anymore 49
　• I don't want my daughter around a dangerous person 49
　If You Haven't Yet Gotten Help 52
　The Pros and Cons List That Helped Me 55
　Plan for Protection 56
　• Security cameras 57
　• Arming yourself 57
　• Documenting events that happen 57
　• Recording calls and threats or issues 57
　• What would help you feel more comfortable in your home? 58
　Following the steps 60
　Breaking HIS Narrative 61
SELF-DISCOVERY 65
　Learning About Your Core Values 65
　Create Your New Core Value System 71
　Role Models and Support Systems 76
　Trusting Again 81
　Rediscovering your passions 82
　It's Okay To Be Selfish 85

 Bumps In The Road 86
Step 3: Mental and Physical Health....................89
 PTSD..91
 Developing Resilience 99
 Autoimmune Diseases 100
THE ROAD AHEAD 103
 Preventative Health.......................................107
 Creating a Healthy Lifestyle For The Next Generation...109
 The Road Ahead 112
LETS CONNECT...116

Chapter One

Learning to Thrive

As I look back at my life overall, all I see is strength. I see someone who would never give up no matter what life threw at her. I see a woman who lived and learned from her mistakes and always tried to be a better version of herself. I have a lot of times where I remember laughing and having a good time and enjoying life.

Those moments are remembered because I try to see the positive moments. Looking back, you have the option to pin-point the positive and only think about those things. When you are living in the bad moments it seems like the bad is a raging river that has sucked you down and won't let you up for air. With every fierce wave it tosses you around with such force that you are just waiting for it to fully break you. With the cards stacked against me growing up in a broken home, having been sexually abused, and then moving away from my family and meeting a Narcissist at the young age of 18, I felt like I was destined for failure.

I had people around me with addictions that covered up their own battles and pain and I refused to go down that road, but sometimes I would catch myself thinking about what my life was really meant to look like. I knew it wasn't a path of self-destruction like I see them doing but what was it?

My daughter once asked me "Mom, why is this happening to me? Why do I have to go through these things?" and the only answer I could give her was "I prayed for a strong girl who could live through any of life's battles and he gave me you". "You are so strong, and you have a little of me in you with the never give up frame of mind so I am sorry that these things are happening, but I will be here right by your side through it all and you will be one tough cookie when it's over." She smiled but still I could see the pain inside of her.

This journey to surviving a narcissist, creating a better life for myself, and eventually using what I had learned to help others has been fulfilling in so many ways. Maybe what I went through is helping me raise a strong, resilient, and driven girl who will never give up in life. Knowing that my story could help just one person out there not give up on life is one of the most precious things I could ever do for someone.

Yes, there is risk in writing this book, as some have pointed out, but the greater risk to me is not helping others out there that are going through the same pains that I did. I want this to give you strength and hope and to guide you to dreaming of and fulfilling a life where you can be strong, stand tall, and rise above trauma.

In the moments of abuse, you feel so damaged, you start to believe what they tell you. You believe you are worthless; you believe you're brainless; you believe you don't have the strength to survive on your own. That's the control that they hold over you, so when you come out the other side, it's like learning to walk when you are a child. You are scared to take the first step but after you do, you feel a sense of accomplishment and keep going and crave more.

You learn to be confident, one little decision at a time. It doesn't matter if it was the fact that you got to choose what grocery store to go to without his judgement or decide which steak to get without wondering what his backlash would be. For me, it was that and then some. Like learning to stand on my own two feet in front of a doctor and demand a resolution when dealing with your health issues.

For years I did not feel competent enough or strong minded enough to even question a doctor let alone demand a resolution. I was blessed because I finally found a doctor that listened to me without judgement. She did not know my deep struggles with a narcissist, my life's traumas, or my fear of questioning authority, but she did know my health struggles and she did everything in her power to help me, even when it put her judgement in question by other doctors and, for that, I thank her. It gave me a fighting chance towards figuring out some very bad health issues.

When you have a support system you get a sense of empowerment and find trust that was hidden deep inside you that you thought was completely stripped away. It doesn't happen overnight, you take it one step at a time, but I never gave up on having a better life, a safer life, and a healthier life.

Take it one step at a time, but never give up on having a better, safer, and happier life.

The Day It Hit Me

When you are in an abusive marriage and you don't have children, it is one thing, but when you do, there is this overwhelming need to protect them that you don't necessarily feel for yourself. I felt like I could handle whatever abuse came at me, but watching my child growing up in this situation, that was a deal breaker.

I was out of town one week and my husband had just driven my eight-month-old daughter seven hours from home to meet me. The second he arrived and stepped out of the truck, I knew he was completely hammered and uncontrollable, and he had put my daughter's life in danger driving that way. We are talking drinking on snowy, icy roads and he couldn't wait until he got there to drink. It was an eye-opener for me.

I thought I could take the abuse, and I did for years, but this was not the kind of life I wanted for my daughter. I remember another time where she was playing with some pots and pans in the kitchen and I was cooking dinner. He came home drunk and cracked open another beer. As I was stirring the food, I could feel myself getting more and more tense. With a narcissist you don't know how the night will end and if you add alcoholism on top of that then it is like an explosion of possibilities, none of which are good. I remember hearing the banging of the pans getting louder and louder until I couldn't take it. I picked my daughter up and took her to the living room floor to play where it wouldn't make as much noise. From the moment he walked in, my nerves were shot, and that is when I knew for a fact that I would be a better mother away from him than I could ever be with him. That moment was when I had short patience with my daughter because of him and that wasn't ok with me.

That was when I started to plan, because with a narcissist, you can never make any hasty decisions. Everything has to be thought out because it is an extremely dangerous situation. That was the moment I realised that I needed a plan to get her to safety. I wanted a better life for her than what I had so far. She had her whole life ahead of her, a big wide world to discover, and it couldn't be limited to alcoholism and narcissism. This was a dangerous, verbally abusive, and destructive environment and I wanted better for her. I had a very destructive upbringing, and I knew firsthand the scars that it can leave on a child.

It was almost a year before I got out because I had to weigh out all of the safety concerns. Would he let me leave? He always said that if I tried to leave then it would be in a pine box. He was so verbally destructive and told me I would never be anything without him and that he would never let me take my daughter. I wondered how would I get out? She was fifteen months old when I finally had the guts to go. This, to me, was the longest, scariest decision.

My mom used to always tell me that she was waiting for THE call and that I would end up on a Dateline show because he had finally taken my life in one of his rages. As you can imagine, she only knew of some things, not all of the things, so that is nerve wracking to hear her say out loud what you already know and fear yourself. Others DO see the abuse too, even when you think they don't. They want you to get out before the unthinkable happens but yet no one wants to help you because they also fear the narcissist and repercussions from him. That is one very lonely and scary spot to be in.

For me, there were steps that I needed to take personally before I could leave. I needed to make sure he was distracted with someone else because then I would not be as big of a target because he would be too busy trying to impress that person to focus on destroying me. I slowly started making decisions that could help me when the time came. I had stashed small amounts of money. I called my family to see if anyone could help me get a lawyer, borrow money, anything. I did not have any support.

Some of my family thinks that no matter what, you never get divorced; others think oh she will figure it out I don't need to help, and the other part of my family just didn't have the money to help me so it took some time for me to actually get to a place where I felt comfortable leaving.

I was alone. I was scared. I had to do this by myself.

If I had a source to help me, I would have left a lot sooner, but when you are on your own and in survival mode, sometimes it takes longer.

For some, they call up mom or dad or whomever is closest to them and they say "Hey come get me, I need help." I didn't have that option and it also didn't help that I lived two states away from my family. Even if they wanted to put a roof over my head, I couldn't leave the state since I shared custody of my daughter. Some judge on how long it took before I actually got out of the bad situation, but some people out there, like me, just didn't have the same support system as others.

Chapter Two

BREAKING OUT

Make a Plan

What did I do to get out? I made a plan. There are certain steps that you need to take when you are in a situation like this. You have a powerful person you are going to trigger and when you don't have the money to go up against him and his wealthy family, you need to make sure you make smart decisions along the way and have things in place before you act on your decisions.

Maybe life isn't about avoiding the bruises. Maybe it is about collecting the scars to prove we showed up for it.
-Author Unknown

Steps that need to be in place:
1. Make sure you have money to be on your own
2. Line up a safe place to live
3. Keep yourself aware of things that he may use against you and make sure to make wise decisions when it comes to your lifestyle

If you don't have it all together when you leave *and* there is a child involved, then there is always the fear that they will try and take your child. Deep down you know you are an amazing mom, and you can provide a great life for your daughter. It doesn't matter how good of a person you are, somehow the narcissist can always get inside of your head and still put those fears in your head that he can prove otherwise.

For me, his narcissist behavior and verbal abuse put fear into me that he would prove that he was the parent that was more fit to have her. He used the money card and said he could provide her a better life. Him and his parents had way more money than I did. I had my love to give her and a simple life and that was not good enough for him. To a narcissist, you are beneath them and not worthy of anything, let alone, raising a child. It was a legit fear that he placed in me that I would lose her to him because I did not have as much money as he did. He threatened for years that he would sue me for full custody, and he said that I would lose her.

So many people said, "Oh he can't do that" and yet the fear was so deep because of how persuasive a narcissist can be. I know there are many people in the same situation out there in the world that need to know that it is ok to take your time to make sure your bases are covered before you get out, because a narcissist can and will destroy you. Be safe, make smart decisions, and have your stuff together before you go, especially if there are kids involved.

Many don't make it out alive. Be aware and be a survivor.

For me, leaving created an entirely new hell. I thought it was bad before, but this was the most heart-wrenching and toughest years of my life.

I knew I would be a better mother part-time and divorced than full-time mom and around him. His abuse made me agitated, fearful, and stressed out, but, most importantly, it was a dangerous situation because he would come home and create a very scary environment and just seemed to look down upon me so much. The verbal abuse was almost unbearable. When would he want to get rid of me? So many times, he would say that he was going kill me and when he says something, he means it. He said that I wasn't worth being his daughter's mom, that I wasn't worth carrying his name, that I wasn't worth anything and that I was trash.

Every time something came up with my daughter, like her getting a cold or her being a little tired, he attributed it to me being a horrible mom. Knowing I could not fight him and take her with me when I left was one of the toughest things I had ever done because I knew how he was and knew she was in danger with his drinking and driving and his violent tendencies. Unfortunately, the justice system doesn't recognize narcissism as a threat and even domestic violence is so hard to prove in the courts.

He was smart, he would not leave a mark, only pure fear. How were they going to give me custody when I couldn't prove anything? I remember one time when I was still married to him, he put me in a choke hold and as I am losing air and pleading with him not to do this again, I thought, tonight is the night that he will not let go and tonight is the night that he will take my life. Those moments happened more times than I like to admit; those are the moments that made me fear him to my core.

Unfortunately, our justice system has so far to come in order to keep us safe. There is so much room for improvement in our justice system to protect people like me and my daughter who deal with a narcissist/alcoholic who thinks their actions are justified and we deserve this treatment. That is why I am wanting to tell people you can survive, you can recover from the abuse, and you can have a beautiful life after the trauma.

Life After the Initial Break-Out

After the immediate plan to get out, there needs to be an ongoing management plan. The hell really started after I left because it was then a fight to keep my daughter safe from afar. Knowing how he was, knowing how he can be, knowing that I could not win against him to get custody because he is so very sly and he is also financially set up to destroy me, I had to do the best I could with what I had and that was the will to survive. The harassment, strong arming, and tear down moments of him picking apart my mothering skills continued for another 12 years. There was a constant battle of him trying to work against me and prove that I was incompetent and unworthy of being my daughter's mom.

Nothing I did was ever good enough: I couldn't dress her well enough, I couldn't feed her good enough, if I gave her chores then I was a cruel mom, and it was abuse. It was always something. I had to make darn sure that every decision that I made in regards to raising her was fool-proof because it would be scrutinized for sure. That is a part of planning.

It was really the last two years when I got the strength to stand up to him again. I saw her breaking down. For years, I was hoping that he was just focusing his abuse onto me, but I saw it changing her; he was verbally tearing her down and things just kept getting worse and worse for her. Every other week when she would come home from his house, she would be more and more broken. I was terrified. I knew this day would come. I knew the day would come that I had to think about how to get her out too.

My choices were

* that I could let things go and risk him drinking and driving with her and having an accident

*him having a rage and emotionally/physically destroying her

*her deciding to stand up to him and him snapping and doing the unthinkable to her

* I could stand up for her and essentially poke the bear and have him do the unthinkable to me and I wouldn't be here to help her anymore (This is something he threatened for years. He always said that he would shoot me in the head and I wouldn't even see it coming)

I was in such a hard situation for so many years. Every week I sent her back to his house, I prayed she would come back safe. Do I stand up to him and poke the bear or do I risk not saying anything until it's too late and something happens to her?

I received full custody when she was 12 years old. There was a breaking point where his actions could no longer be feared; I had to do something. For those of you out there that think there is no hope, there is. Just keep going one day at a time and keep moving in a positive direction in your life so that you are there when your children need you the most. I had to set my fears of him aside and put her first. She was at her breaking point with him and she couldn't take his verbal abuse anymore. I knew that it was time.

This book is not here to discuss her or what she went through other than to explain a narcissists abuse is not biased; they abuse everyone in their path. For those of you wondering why did it take so long? Why was she in his care so long if he was dangerous and destroying her? Well, this is where the scars that built me comes in because it was not an easy road. For me, during those years, there was no other way.

Until I was financially set up to fight him, until I had all of my ducks in a row to prove his abuse, and until I was healed enough myself to have a backbone to fight him, it just wasn't something that could have happened sooner. Narcissists are very careful, methodical, and can abuse you and no one around you will ever be the wiser. That being said, I had to rely on other people to keep her safe when she was in his care. I knew his girlfriends were moms too and they would watch out for her. I knew his parents always came to his rescue when he was drinking way too much and yelling and screaming and scaring my daughter. They would go pick her up and she would stay with them. So, it was not like I just let things be for 12 years, it is just that I had other resources to keep an eye on her and I knew she was at least ok some of the time and that would get me through.

Everyone talks about divine timing and for me it just all fell together to where I had a good support system, I could financially fight him, and I also had what I needed to prove without a doubt that she needed to come live with me full time. Today, she is a strong, beautiful 14-year-old who no longer wants to give up on life. Unfortunately, that 12-year-old did want to give up because a narcissist can make you feel so unworthy that life just seems too hard. When I saw that hopeless mindset take over my daughter, I no longer feared him; I had to step up and help her regardless of the consequences.

Many of us going through this think we can't fight them; they will win. We leave our children in that situation and pray for the best. We settle. I never wanted to settle. I wanted her to know that life didn't have to be that way, but I just didn't know how to help her without facing the man I feared so much and making her life with him worse. Poking the bear, as I thought of it. The point I want to get across to you is that if you never ever give up, your time will come, you will rise above, and you can recover from the trauma and so can your children. It may be a long road but keep going.

There are millions of people out there who grow up with an alcoholic narcissistic father who are probably fine or have support systems that keep them from being fully destroyed, she wasn't one of those. She had me but only every other week and the weeks with him overpowered all other good moments.

There is no force equal to a woman determined to rise.

-Author Unknown

In my gut I knew I needed to get her out of there. She was being broken down, she was getting so angry, she was giving up on life at such a young age. She was being mentally broken. He got enraged and said some things that truly crossed the line. He took the target off my back and put it on hers. Enough is enough. I planned all these years and I did it as safely and strategically as I could, but it all came to a head one day and that day was THE day. I never gave up, EVER. I knew that someday I would be able to get her out of there and into a safe place. You just need to never lose faith.

Never Ever Give Up

I was going to call this book *Never EVER Give Up* because it truly was a very long journey and overcoming multiple things that most people would have probably given up, but I didn't. Years of abuse and years of trying just to survive and pray someday he would leave us alone. First reason to name it "The Scars That Built Me" was there were so many deep emotional scars created along the way and it has been a lifelong battle for me to heal from and I know it will be for her also.

Never give up; the best is yet to come

The scars are deep. Scars heal over, but they are always there to remind you what you have been through. The title of this book touches me on so many levels. I have mental scars from him and she has them physically and mentally. I feel deep inside my soul I'm scarred but those scars are what truly made me who I am today and I used them as a stepping stone and not as concrete to weigh me down.

What is a narcissist?

A narcissist is a person who builds up the people they are around. They are very charismatic, outgoing, and funny to the public. They put on a persona of being very successful, powerful, funny, and happy-go-lucky. But, they have a hidden sense of control over everyone around them. His friends fear him but have a weird sense of devotion to him. A narcissist behind closed doors is a very negative person and will tear people down behind their backs. Nothing is ever good enough for them, they will find something to pick apart about everyone and everything.

They have a sense of emptiness that needs fulfilled. It could be anything from having to always buy the latest, greatest snowmobile, to always wanting to have the biggest, best house. They are always trying to find something to make themselves happy but most importantly they are building themselves up above everyone else who they view as worthless.

Add alcoholism in there and you have what I call "a rock falling from the sky" moment where the person goes from fine and happy to dark-eyed and angry. Statistics show 1 in 3 women have experienced some form of violence by an intimate partner and 1 in 7 women have been injured by an intimate partner every year. What is associated to that is approximately 5 million children a year are exposed to domestic violence situations. Take that information and put it together with the decision you are trying to make about leaving. Although it gives you confirmation on needing to get out, it makes the decision of how to get out a lot harder.

Narcissist abuse is the psychological, financial, sexual and physical abuse of others and has been referred to as a mental health condition

A narcissist believes in themselves more than any other human. If they have to cause harm or damage to others, they feel 100% justified. I remember this one time that my husband came home drunk, was mad at the world, drug me out of bed and put a gun to my head because I was unworthy of him. The next day when I reminded him of what he did the night before when he was intoxicated, he acted like he was fully justified in doing so. He says he doesn't remember those actions but yet he had this what did you do to piss me off attitude about him that told me otherwise.

There were so many other things that were detrimental to people's well-being and he always felt 100% justified in his actions. We are always beneath them. We are peasants and they are the king. They feel no matter what you do or what you say, you are always beneath them and they can treat you however they feel fit.

I don't know anyone personally in my friends' group who has been through the same types of things as me, but I know there are millions of people out there going through it. I follow support groups for these situations and there are so many lives affected by a narcissist's actions. Not just a wife or a child but family members, friends, and co-workers.

People in my situation tend to stay silent for a long time. Mostly because if you speak the words and start saying all of the things that happened them it almost seems surreal. It seems fake, it seems exaggerated and it seems like there is no possible way someone could do those things and get away with it but most of the time it just seems so very unbelievable. When you are broken emotionally and have had your mind toyed with for so long, it is hard to actually have faith that people could believe this treacherous story of your life.

Narcissism is very real, very scary, and creates a hell that no one can even comprehend unless you have been in it yourself. The world needs to know about narcissism. It is a true mental disease they have no control over and there are victims like myself and my daughter that need the justice system to step up and help us long before it causes the kind of heartache that it led to in my life where he tore my daughter down to the point of giving up.

The justice system and the courts need to figure out a way to help people like me and I want this book to change lives. For example, he has terrorized me for so many years, but the justice system says until he caused that 100% harm, or physical harm, there was nothing the court system could do. The fear and mental trauma that a narcissist causes is not recognized enough in the world. I want people to understand it is real, it is scary, and it is causing so much harm to so many people. Either the people living with the trauma give up or it ends up in a domestic violence situation where people get killed.

Narcissism is a very dangerous disease. I want you to know that no matter what, you can always recover, you can always move forward, and you can learn to thrive after the abuse. In my case, as mentioned before, this went on for many, many years. Look at me now: I now have confidence again and I am thriving so don't give up. You can get here too.

Isolation

Part of the control is to isolate you from your family, friends, and even co-workers. I feel even if you were around your family, friends, and co-workers, they wouldn't actually believe the hell you are living through. You don't mention it. You don't want to talk about it. It is dramatic and something people think is exaggerated. Sometimes you slide a comment out just to see how people take it but most of the time you just feel so broken that you don't even mention it.

When I was living through it, I felt like I was 100% alone and had nobody to reach out to, which is how he wanted me to feel. Being the black sheep of the family, childhood traumas that scar you and then add this abuse and well you just don't really feel like there is any help out there for you. Life has worked against you for so long that sometimes that loneliness seems to be never ending.

Narcissists are wicked smart. For example, at a party one time he would pull me aside where no one could see, keep his voice low, and say some very damaging things to me. Then he would walk out and smile to the group of people standing there and act as if nothing was wrong. I would try to pull myself together, not cry, and pretend like everything was fine. Sometimes I could pull it off and sometimes I couldn't.

If someone asked him what was wrong with me, he would say, "Oh, she's just having a moment," or he would discount it and turn it on me. He was also building a relationship with others around me by making me appear as crazy. They will always make sure that you look like the bad guy.

Freedom of your mind and body is something that you have. You just have to remember that you hold the key to your freedom and your happiness. This is where the steps come in. If you want to change something, you have to take that step forward in order to make the change. It requires work on your part but if you have the drive, the want, the fight in you to survive then you can change your circumstances in life then you can do it with these steps.

Chapter Three

THE STEPS TO SURVIVAL

Step 1- Assessment and Planning

Assessment is what keeps you alive during the process. If I walked away without thinking of the consequences, it would have gotten very dangerous, very fast. You have to write a plan, get things organized, and have a back-up plan. What house are you going to go to? You have to rebuild your life by yourself. You have to have things in place in order to do that.

A turning point for me was drawing up a pros and cons list. What are the pros of leaving the marriage, and what are the cons of staying in it. It is finding out you can and will get through it, you just have to follow these steps to get there. That is where the assessment comes in handy.

If you were to just throw out a comment, or want to pack your things and leave, you would start a war. You are a controlled person; they will take advantage of everything they try to make sure that you don't have anywhere to go or anyone to turn to, so you need to be aware of that. They will use those things against you and when a child is involved you can't risk not having all of your stuff lined up in every possible way as to not give them any ammo.

The pros and cons list is about getting a clear picture of where you are now, and where you want to be, then developing some strategies to move to the next level. How do you want to change your life? What are the things you are going to allow in your life? What are the things you don't want in your life? How are you going to get there? What are your must-haves and what are your negotiables?

Pros (good) and Cons (Bad) list example

What do you want IN your life	What do you want GONE from your life
Peace	Fear
Positivity	Abuse
Happiness	Negativity
Energy	Anger
Confidence	Resentment
Hope	Alcoholism

Step 2 - Self Discovery and Learning About Your Core Values

The biggest thing I realized was I didn't know who I was. I lost my core values. I was ashamed of who I was. I used to have core values instilled in me from one of my most influential family members and I had lost them. I sacrificed myself along the way to avoid fights and lost those values. I had to go back, really sit down and think about it. That was my self-discovery.

I am not a victim. No matter what I have been through, I am still here. I have a history of victory.

-Dr Steve Maraooli

The mental trauma caused by him had a bigger reach on me than I realized. When I went to a doctors appointment, I felt insecure. What if they asked me questions? Was I giving them the right answers? Would they look down on me for not knowing simple things? It was the same thing at work. I always felt insecure about the work I was doing. How were others viewing it? I felt so scrutinized by him that I couldn't even make a decision like deciding if I wanted to go to a barbeque or not with my daughter. What would he think? He would find something negative about what I was doing and who I was doing it with and I just couldn't do anything without stressing about that. I felt scrutinized, even though I probably wasn't half the time, but that is how you feel once they harass you for that long. Trust me, they let you know about everything you do that they don't approve of.

Discovering who you are and who you want to be and coming up with a real list of goals for improving your life and healing is the biggest step to starting your recovery.

Step 3 - Health and Wellbeing is Important

Because you are so busy fighting to stay alive and dig yourself out of the deep hell you are in, you lose your health along the way. It starts with your mental health, and the stress that puts on your body, then goes to your physical health.

There are multiple reports showing trauma causes autoimmune disease. The life and freedom you fought so hard for get knocked out from underneath you.

If I could go back and take better care of my health leading up to leaving, I would. I know some things are out of our hands, but it is a repercussion that really knocks you down. You are finally out of this hell and want to live a better life, but you don't have the strength to do it. It is super important you plan to either go to counselling to help support your mental health, or go to a doctor for any physical issue you have before you hit a brick wall.

If you don't make time for your health now, you will be forced to make time for your illness later

- Author Unknown

The consequences of not paying attention to these three things is really powerful. If your health and wellbeing step is not sorted out, you won't have strength. If your self-discovery step is not sorted out, you have no hope. If your assessment step is not sorted out, it feels like there is no way out.

From the Outside Looking In

My friends didn't know why I acted the way that I did, and they had no clue the pain that I was going through. They thought I was living a happy life, the high life. That is the persona he created, he had them fooled.

There is always money involved with narcissism. They like to flaunt it, and in my husband's case, money is important. Some of my friends and family felt abandoned; like I was living the high life and moving on without them.

That wasn't it at all. It was control. He had me locked down so much with who I could talk to. When and if I went out with friends, he controlled the situation and harassed me to the point I didn't want to go because it wasn't worth the issues. At that point people started giving up on me. They thought I didn't want to go out with them, but it wasn't them, it was because the repercussions were so bad.

You Are The Prey

Narcissists prey on the weak. Unfortunately, I had some trauma in my closet he picked up on, and he knew I could be easily controlled. I was looking for someone to be a support system, give me advice, and be that person for me. He took advantage of that and built me up. He put me on a pedestal and told me all the good things about me. He taught me things, whether it was jet boating, hooking up and pulling trailers, all kinds of things to make me feel good about myself and make me feel empowered. He bragged about me and the things I could do and always talked me up with our friends in certain times and they would forget about the moments he tried to make me seem crazy and all they took away from the experience was that he worships me. Wrong. Just as easily as he built me up, he would knock my feet out from under me and crush me.

We were always putting on events and parties and in front of others he just put me so high up. That's why it was so traumatic behind closed doors, because I was so confused. He said to all the others that I was the greatest person in the world, so why was he tearing me down when they were not around? Why does he do the, she is amazing...she is crazy...back and forth stuff? It is a life of games.

There were a few good years there that were really good, because he lies to create a sense of happiness that is false. There was a real disconnect between what it looked like from the outside and what was going on in the inside. There was a disconnect between how he spoke about me publicly, then what he said to me privately. It broke my resistance, it broke my spirit, and it broke my soul.

It also broke my sense of reality. If I mentioned to a friend or someone there was anything unhappy going on in our home, they wouldn't believe it because he spoke so highly of me in public. They couldn't fathom why I was unhappy in the relationship, or why I feared him because he put on one hell of a show.

Many narcissists are charismatic, fun to be around, and on the surface, they look very appealing. They strategically operate in a way that makes you trust them. Then they create a disconnect between what is happening publicly and privately. Then they create a control system, and that is how they get you.

The Second-Guessing Game

You start second guessing reality. You break down the situations in your head and wonder what you could have done differently. What could I have done not to set him off? What could I have done to fix the situation? What can I do in the future to avoid this situation? I remember distinctly this one time that I said that was a good-looking black truck over there. He said that was white. I said no that truck we just passed. It was black. With a very disgusted look on his face, he stated it was white and that it wasn't good looking at all. Knowing that it was the only vehicle on the road at the time I knew it was black but at that moment I caught myself thinking and questioned myself, it was black, right? At that moment I realized his power. To many that seems like just a misspoken mistake or that

I am taking the topic too far, but it is not. It is a complete control over your mind. It wasn't as if the vehicle was a dark grey and we were discussing a slight color difference, we were literally discussing black and white and he made me second guess what I clearly knew was black.

You become a pleaser. But to a narcissist, being a pleaser is a sign of weakness. They start seeing you as weak and start moving down the road of wanting to dispose of you because they feel you are even more worthless. They feel you don't meet their standards any longer. They have broken you down so much that they no longer think you are worthy of their time.
They want you weak and they want to control you, but yet they don't respect that. They don't necessarily want to get rid of you at that point, but there is just such a lack of respect, the abuse gets worse and worse because they are frustrated with the way things are now. This is when they move on and target others.

It's Not Just Intimate Partners

The second place I saw narcissism was in the workplace. They like to hold big positions and control others and a workplace is where they can control many. I had a boss who was a narcissist and recognized it immediately. It was easy for me to spot the red flags, but the boss reeled me in with money and promises of my dream job. After they seal the deal, they start the tear down process. The boss also made me so dependent on them financially, that the boss felt they could break me and I would take it because they had control over me financially.

Building you up, making you dependent, then isolating you to the point where you feel you have no strength, occurs the same way, whether it is in a personal relationship or a work environment. For me, this time around, it was easy to recognize and easy to walk away from before things got too bad. Money is never worth your peace of mind. There are always other opportunities out there for you so don't give up and stay in a bad environment.

Chapter Four

THE HELP YOU NEED

Facts vs Feelings

The best way, and it is not easy, to figure out your assessment is to separate facts versus your feelings. You can feel like he hates you and you are worthless, but those are not reality. That is your perception of the situation you are in because you are made to believe that. Reality is, worthless is a feeling and facts are that you are not. You need to break down your best qualities and know what you are good at and not let someone change your thoughts about it. Maybe you went to college and got a bachelor's degree and continued to get your doctorate. That reality is you are a smart, intelligent person. Maybe you didn't go to college, but you are successful in your job. You need to go through all those things and discard the feeling or emotion of the situation and just look at the facts and not feel bad about it.

What are the facts?

- I don't want this style of life anymore
- I don't want the danger factor in my life anymore
- I don't want my daughter around a dangerous person

Those facts are real. Those situations have happened. It is dangerous. That word is real. Scary is a feeling, dangerous is a fact. Perception is that you can't find a resolution and that you feel like there is no way out.

Write the facts in one area and write the perceptions or feelings in another area. Keep the perceptions separate and focus on moving forward with the fact list.

If you can, go and talk to a counsellor, give them all the details, and ask them to help you separate your list. It can be extremely difficult to do on your own. It can take outside help to distinguish between the two.

"Asking for help is a sign of strength not weakness"

Hebrews 4:16

I discussed my story with a counsellor and expressed my concerns. I wanted to validate whether I was exaggerating or whether it was a real problem. I wanted to make sure that was clear in my head before I made any hasty decisions. Given my situation and the events that occurred, they told me I was on the right path, my gut was telling me it was dangerous, and I should remove myself from the situation.

At first that validation tore me in half because I realized, I was not crazy, and was in a very bad situation. It really smacked me in the head. Even though I lived it already, it was like confirming my fears a second time around. It is a little hard to swallow sometimes because it feels like when you go back and revisit the traumas and the heartache, you realise it was real and terrifying to go through.

Up until that point, you are living it, but you have not got the diagnosis of him being a narcissist. You haven't had someone confirm that is what is happening, you are in a dangerous situation, and you need to do something about it but you need more concrete evidence also.

It rocked me. It confirmed how dangerous the situation was. Then I started to fear the future and whether it would get worse or not based on my decision on whether to stay or leave. It was a confirmation of an extremely dangerous situation, but it was a bit gratifying because it confirmed what I thought in my head.

He controlled my every thought and made me question every decision; he made me feel so weak, and so dumb, and so incompetent; that final breakthrough moment was a kind of validation. It was a little like mending my heart because I realized, I was not crazy. I was not making up a bad situation, exaggerating, or blowing it out of proportion. I got a sense of my own brain back. It is the first step to really knowing you have made it to the other side, you are on your way to recovery, you are on your new journey, and your whole life can start over from this point.

If You Haven't Yet Gotten Help

I know when you are in it, it feels like there is no possible way you are ever going to be mended or happy. You feel so broken and unworthy that you can't see how life could be anything but hard. Don't ever settle.

The enemy doesn't stand a chance when the victim decides to survive

-Rae Smith

Don't think what is happening to you is ok, because it is not. There is happiness for everyone out there in the world. Have a bit of faith and hope and you can get through it, just don't give up on yourself.

By investing your time, seeking and accepting help, whether it is just an outsider to confirm what is happening and helping you see you can create another life, you can do it. I know what it is like to feel trapped and not see any options, but don't give up. Things can always get better. It may take time, but it will get better.

Start planning your new life now. Unless you invest in yourself, you can't find a way out. Research programs or places that can help you. I personally know that before I got out and before I got help, it was a miserable life. I could see the positive sometimes. I could smile and laugh but no one knew the hell I was living. The traumas that were being done to me and the horrific verbal abuse that was occurring. To some, it is still hard for them to comprehend, to others they say yes that man scares me too.

The Pros and Cons List That Helped Me

I felt like this black cloud was following me everywhere I went until I did my pros and cons list. One of my counsellors introduced it to me and I feel everyone should do a pros and cons list with anything in their life that they are having a hard time with; especially when they are younger. It is such a great tool to help you make those hard decisions that life throws at you.

I got together with my husband when I was 18. At that age you don't know who you are, and this is something that can help you define yourself. Do you want alcoholism and rage in your life, or don't you? What is your picture of a happy life? What does it look like without him? Would you be happier without him?

It breaks down what you think about in your head all the time. Writing it and seeing it on a piece of paper is something totally different. Once I wrote it down and actually saw the cons for staying with him were way longer that the pros for staying with him, I realized that was a problem. It was a real eye opener.

When I wrote that pros and cons list of leaving or staying, it was like that black cloud hanging over me for so long parted. It was literally like looking up at the sky and seeing it parting and the sun coming out after a rainstorm. That moment gave me a sense it was going to be okay. I was making the right decision.

It is really two lists:
1. What you want in your life and what you don't want in your life
2. Can that person give you that or not if they are in your life

Writing what I wanted in my life really gave me a sense of everything I didn't want in my life. Everything I didn't want in my life was on the list with him in it. If I eliminated him, I eliminated half of my fears, struggles, stress, and dangers.

Plan for Protection

If you don't make a plan, you will always be looking over your shoulder, you will always live in fear, and the narcissist will still control you. One of the things to heal yourself, is to eliminate those fears by planning to protect yourself. Whether it is learning to use a gun, putting security cameras in your house, or getting the appropriate authorities to know your story and back you up should it come up again.

Step 1. Write a list of what will make you feel safe
- Security cameras
- Arming yourself
- Documenting events that happen
- Recording calls and threats or issues

These are examples of what I did for myself, but you need to make a plan for yourself to increase how safe you feel.

It is a difficult step for some of us to comprehend. I always thought of guns as a negative because of the way he used them, but it was a step I needed to take based on the threats he made towards me. It was like I evolved into the new me. I was inspired by a movie called ENOUGH. I saw the power that she had to survive within her and how she overcame her fears and took the precautions that she needed to take to keep herself and her daughter safe. She made an exit plan, secured her new house with things to keep her safe and she got the protection training that she needed to survive another attack if it happened.

It was emotional and gave me a sense of security where I could breathe on my own. I could live comfortably in my house without drawing the shades, I could sit near windows knowing I had a warning system to alert me long before he could be standing there, and I could have my back to the door which was not even a consideration before. This step gives you a plan to help you get rid of your fears and feel more comfortable in life.

Here are some questions to ask yourself.

- What would help you feel more comfortable in your home?
- Would it help you feel more comfortable if you had a camera facing the driveway where you knew someone was coming before they were here?

It helps to come up with a plan to face it head on and give you a sense of peace.

Above all be the heroine of your life, not the victim

-Nora Ephron

Following the steps

In my head, I knew I couldn't take my daughter with me full-time, and I knew I had to get myself out. My plan was to get out and heal myself so I was strong enough and coherent enough to fight to help her. I thought if I was broken and weak fighting my own battles, then I couldn't stand up for her. I knew he wouldn't release her easily. I needed to get my own house, I needed my own additional income, and I needed to build a life where no matter what he told the courts or anybody, I knew I was a good mother and had a supportive household for her to grow up in.

I needed to create the situation where no one on God's earth could say I had an unfit home, because that was what he would and did preach. I planned to create this amazing lifestyle for her so I could then take the steps I needed to get her out safely and have a good, stable, and healthy home versus the other.

It was like when you travel on a plane with a child and they tell you to fit your own oxygen mask first, because if you are not breathing, you can't help that child. If you put it on the child first and pass out, you are no good to them. I needed to fit my oxygen mask first so I could care for my child and move her out of the situation as well.

Breaking HIS Narrative

It was really important for me to create a clear, fact-based situation so when anyone looked at it, they could see what he said had no resemblance on what they saw. I wanted the freedom to go out and do things and not be judged. I didn't want everything I did used against me. I had to pick my battles so what did I want more in life? I wanted my daughter to be safe, and I didn't want to give him any ammunition to use in any way so I tried every single day to make better and better decisions in my life and well for that I need to thank him because I refused to give up or give in and I constantly showed up as a mother and was the best I could be.

You need to choose where you live and the people you surround yourself with wisely if you don't want the narcissist to tear you a part for your decisions.

When I left, he took everything from me. He kept all of my precious belongings and all of her keepsakes. I literally walked out with very minimal items. I didn't have as much money as him, which was a point of harassment by him and his family. According to them I was not up to par.

My first thought was I needed to get out, and I would figure out the rest as far as a home went. The cute little two-bedroom house I quickly learned was not good enough for them, and they threw it back in my face. It shouldn't have been as big of an issue because I was a struggling Mom trying to rebuild myself and couldn't afford the big, fancy house on the canyon he could, but the moment I got a house that was at a higher standard, not like I needed his approval, it gave him zero things to throw back at me. Well, about living conditions anyway.

Don't give them any reasons to tear you down. You need to plan for a good home, a good income, and a job that will support your family so, if possible, you don't need any outside help. Plan out your home life, your work life, your child's day care, your child's home life, your support networks, and so on. They are watching.

You yourself, as much as anybody in the entire universe, deserve your love and affection

- Buddha

Chapter Five

SELF-DISCOVERY

Learning About Your Core Values

After a narcissist's abuse, you get lost along the way and forget who you are, where you came from, and the core values you have. You swayed into their world of what they think is right and what they think is wrong. You lose that sense of what you feel is truly right or wrong.

Starting your journey or relearning who you are, it is important to sit down and figure out what your core values are.

- How are you as a family person?

- How do you want to raise your children?
- What are you doing at work?
- Will you go to college?
- Are you going to cheat the system, or are you going to do it correctly?
- Who do you want to be?
- What actions make you feel proud of yourself?
- What actions don't? (these are the ones to get rid of)

You need to know who you are inside. For me it was a journey. I had gotten loose minded with my actions and started to not care about my actions or words because I was so numb that it just didn't matter anymore. I most importantly started making decisions and doing things that made me not feel good with who I was. This I knew needed to change. I could not be like him; I was better than that. I needed to find my core values again.

That was really important for me. I grew up in a world where your spoken word was your word. A handshake was a handshake. I lost that along the way and had to take a step back and remember how good it felt to stand by my core values. Even if it was something small like if I said I was going to be somewhere at a certain time, then I was there at that time. If I said I was going to help a friend, I went and helped that friend. I wasn't flaky and I didn't give excuses. I stood up tall and was a very proud person and I was proud of my actions. I was that person until I lost those core values and I wanted them back.

Self Discovery Worksheet

Who are you?

1. What brings you joy?

2. What brings you heartache and stress?

3. What are your best qualities?

4. What are your worst qualities?

5. How is your health?

6. How do you want your health to be?

When dealing with a narcissist, it is super easy to try and keep the peace in that moment. "If you can't beat them, join them." He was an alcoholic, so I thought maybe if I drank with him, we would have a good time. Maybe if I loosened up like he always told me, we would have a good time. Even after the divorce I told myself it is ok to go and have some beverages and have fun and let loose like he does. Wrong. It is not something that makes you feel good and that wasn't really who I wanted to be. In those moments when I stooped to his level, consumed the alcohol to be that person he said he wanted me to be, the alcohol made me into not a very nice person either. I remember making really bad choices under the influence. It was good for him because he was proving that he was right, I was less than worthless. It was really bad for me, because it wasn't who I was inside. I would let my bad decisions eat away at me and interrupt my recovery.

It didn't make me feel very good and I wasn't a drinker to begin with. When I took that leap and followed his lead, it took me to a dark place I didn't want to be in. My main goal when I left was to be an amazing mom, person, employee, friend, new wife someday, etc. THAT put me back on track.

It was a very lost, lonely, and humiliating point in my life when I was not caring. I figured I have been through so much in my life that I deserve to not care for a while. That is the place that I do not want anyone to be in. I knew I was better than that, and I didn't want to be like him.

I wasn't that person inside and my heart and soul were on a different path. I picked myself up once again and told myself you can do this. You can surpass anyone's expectations of who you are, and you can THRIVE. I know it so let's go do it and find those core values and start our journey.

She remembered who she was and the game changed.

- Author Unknown

Create Your New Core Value System

The best way to create your value system is step-by-step. Create this ladder and use the information you have as the first step.

STEP 1: That action didn't make me feel very good inside.
STEP 2: What am I going to do about it? Well, I'm going to cut those things out of my life and push them to a place where they no longer affect me and make better decisions.
STEP 3: Repeat the process. This didn't make me feel good, what is going to help me rise above that?
STEP 4: Use the information learned to stack up and help me get up to the next step in my ladder

Stairs to thriving

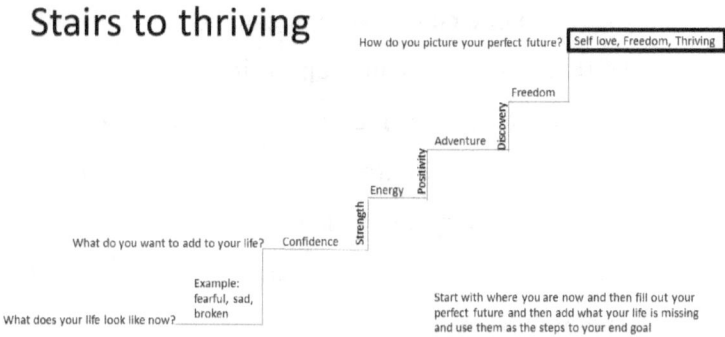

The pros and cons list gave me the main highlighted topics that I needed to evaluate. I then took the information and wrote it out in what looked like a ladder. It was a tool for me to rise above, and it helped that it looked like a ladder. I wanted to reach the top. You go step by step, in order, and start doing the things that make you feel positive inside instead of negative. When you get to the top, you can shine.

"Truth" was an important value for me when I started this process. You learn ways to keep yourself safe and one of those things puts you in positions where you have to lie in order to not set off the narcissist. It was always a hidden factor. He came off as happy-go-lucky and some people would say he had a bad side to him however no one could ever imagine how bad it really was. If someone brought it up, or if someone saw me hurting and they asked me about it, I would lie to cover it up by saying things are fine he is just drunk. If they knew the true story and called him out on it, it would make my world worse. I remember one time that a friend of mine caught him doing some not so favourable things and confronted him. He was so mad. I had no clue why he all of a sudden didn't want me hanging out with her anymore. It got to the point where I cut her out of my life just to keep peace at home.

Here I was bending those core values and found myself in the middle of this world where I would lie to cover up his actions for him. I remember this one time that I had a surgery and stitches and he was driving so recklessly and angrily that he ripped my stitches out. When I had to go back to the doctor, I said I must have done it and didn't know how.

It became a way of life of instantly putting out the lie versus the truth because I was scared of what would happen and the anger that would arise out of him if I said something wrong or if he got in trouble for something. That wasn't who I was or wanted to be. The person I grew up with that had the most influence on me when it came to core values was my grandpa. He instilled truth telling in me and I wanted to go back to that. His name meant something and his word meant something. He was who I looked up to the most. He was a hard-working proud man who took care of his family. That is who I wanted to be and that is what I wanted to go back to.

When I started living that value it was terrifying. I had to face the fact that I was dishonest and people no longer trusted me like they did before when they found out the truth. I never once lied about the abuse that I went through and I never lied about the trauma that was created but it was other things in life that I was not truthful about. I was not truthful in my future relationships because I was constantly trying to cover up this broken person that I was. I feared telling the truth sometimes and really had no reason to in the current situation. They were not HIM.

Facing your own actions that you aren't proud of is terrifying. Deep down I knew I was a good-hearted person. This is where your self-discovery and self-worth comes into play. This is what needs built back up. This is a part of your journey of going from broken and afraid to confident and thriving.

Don't let your bad decisions haunt you for life; learn from them.

- Angela Newhouse

Self-discovery gives you a sense of freedom like no other. It is like being suffocated and then finally getting your air back. I remember one of the times when my ex-husband had choked me during the relationship so bad that I felt like I was going to never get air again. The moment he released my neck was a feeling I will never forget. When I discovered myself again and became truly happy with who I was, it was like that moment of freedom when I got my air back. It gave me a sense that life was going to be ok.

Role Models and Support Systems

I had a rough childhood growing up and I didn't have very good role models within that system. When I turned to look at my daughter, I wanted to be a role model for her. That was the number one defining moment where I knew I needed to turn things around and get myself healed. She needed me to be strong. She needed me to stand up for her. She needed a MOM and I was determined to not let the trauma created by my last marriage give her a broken mom. I wanted this long line of abuse, bad decisions, heart ache and trauma to STOP with me. I wanted her to have a better life and

I knew first-hand how much childhood trauma can affect you for a large portion of your life and I am starting NOW to heal myself and help her heal herself also.

I had someone come into my life who was very positive. I don't know how I got blessed with meeting him or how the chemistry worked so hard in our favour, but I am thankful every day. He pointed out the good things in me, lightened up the hardened parts of me and also helped me find who I wanted to be. One thing that he taught me that has truly healed me in so many ways was to tell me to find a hobby and find what I am passionate about. What things am I passionate about? I didn't even know because I had put my passions aside for so long.

Without that particular role model in my life, I wouldn't have taken the steps to finish the self-discovery, to finish figuring out what my passions were and to have a drive to always learn more and more ways to be a better person that is not so hard and broken. Without these steps that I am laying out, the road to thriving is much harder.

Turn your wounds into wisdom

-Oprah Winfrey

Having a positive mentor or role model is such an amazing experience because it gives you the ability to not only think outside the box, but have an outsider looking in. Sometimes we are blinded to our good parts and we can't see any good in ourselves. They can help us through that. That really helped me get to where I am today. He was fun, lighthearted, creating so much laughter that my life for sure needed. Through my healing process he stuck in there and I know it wasn't easy for him.

He is my current husband and he believed in me so much, gave me so much positivity, and pushed and pushed me to dive deep and find my passions. For example, I got back into a hobby I had a long time ago of riding horses. It was like therapy for me, and to have him backing me 110% while I was still having flashbacks to traumas, was very inspiring. I saw the kind of person he was and knew that was a good example I wanted to pass down to the next generations. He gave my daughter a loving father figure to respect and learn from and created an environment that was non-threatening and that was a safe place to heal. He did not take the place of her father but was there to show the many positive ways that a family could interact.

With every passing day he helped put me back together and made life more beautiful than I could ever imagine.

- Angela Newhouse

Trusting Again

When your trust is completely broken, one of the hardest things to do is move forward with your life, collect those new positive moments, put the negative ones in a jar with a lid on them, and be secure enough to trust another person. That is not just in your personal life with a partner, it goes for family members, and in your work life, because when you are in all of this negativity, you tend to instantly get defensive and try to protect yourself from any further harm.

If anyone tells you that you are doing something wrong, you are so hard pressed that you haven't done anything wrong and HE did that. Then you start to realize you are fighting a ghost. But you are broken and sometimes it is hard to see that yourself. You have had opinions shoved in your head for so long that you can't think for yourself. When you find a mentor or that positive person in your life, you need to take that time when they give you a suggestion and just breathe and collect your thoughts before instantly putting your guard up. I call it "*woosah-ing*." I learned it from one of my favorite movies. It just kind of spoke to me. It was humorous but it got the point across to me that when you are in a high stressful situation, you stop, take a deep breath, and *woosah*. It stuck with me from that day forward.

Another way that I learned to view it was to think about trust as a giant jar of jellybeans. Each time someone does something positive, or there is an agreement they kept, it's like you are putting a few more jellybeans in the jar. The ongoing relationship of trust is like continuing to fill up that jar.

Occasionally they might do something that destroys a little bit of that trust and that means you take a few jellybeans out of the jar. It doesn't mean you upend the entire jar of jellybeans and never trust them again. It is a continual process of depositing elements of trust. Occasionally there will be withdrawals, but the trend should be building it up overtime.

Rediscovering your passions

Rediscovering my passions was like walking out into the sunshine for the first time in the Spring when it is warm outside. That sun hits your face, you take a big breath of fresh air, and the sun on your face is a feeling like no other. It puts a smile on your face. When you lose your passions, you don't realise it. When you are in survival mode, you don't pay attention to your wants or needs, you put everybody else ahead of you. Rediscovering your passions is like opening a new present at Christmas and seeing that what is in there can change your life and make your world better.

It is like having a second chance at life and it can go in any direction you want. Sitting down and rediscovering what you're passionate about, that you lost along the way, is like rebirth. It is your new journey. You are starting all over again. You deserve it so give it all you got!

My passion was riding horses. I had to start again at ground zero. Yes, I was passionate about it, but I had to learn things all over again. It was terrifying, but also fulfilling. With each step you learn, and every maneuver or adventure you go on, it teaches you to get over your fears. Maybe you are terrified to go on a trail ride because you haven't ridden in years. It teaches you to trust your horse and to trust your abilities.

It taught me to put everything aside and focus on just me and the horse together, our bond, and taking those steps together to move forward. It doesn't matter if your passion is horses or painting, you have to take those first steps and throw yourself into it.

You are going to hit bumps along the road, you are going to hit new fears, but if you're passionate about it, it will be a driving force because you love it so much, you're not going to quit. Coming from a world where you were stopped all the time and couldn't think for yourself, when you have such a positive reinforcement and drive for something you're passionate about, it makes the healing process ten times faster.

One of the things unique about any passion is you become extremely present. As a victim of a narcissistic relationship, you are often caught up in your mind about past things that happened, or anxious about the future, not dealing with what is happening right here and now. Dealing with the present helps you become who you would like to be. Passion is really about blocking out the past, ignoring the future, and being mindful about the activity you're doing. As long as that activity is exciting and interesting for you, it doesn't matter what it is. That is a powerful force for healing.

It's Okay To Be Selfish

You need to put your oxygen mask on you before you help someone else, otherwise you are of no use to them. Unless you heal yourself and are a little bit selfish, you are not going to be any good to anyone else. You are not going to heal, you will go right back into the same train of thought, hang with the same type of people, and be around the same traumas.

It is 100% necessary to be a little selfish, even though it is one of the hardest steps. It is setting a good example for the next generation. I wanted to be a better person for her, and unless I was a little bit selfish and took the time out I needed to take, she wasn't going to see the great things I have to offer. She wasn't going to see the wonderful me, she was going to see the traumatised me. As much as I was scared of that step, and as much as I felt like I didn't deserve to take that step, it was a necessary step to take. You have to heal yourself before you can help others.

You need to change your mindset or reprogram your mind to see that healing yourself is a necessary step and it is not really selfish.

Bumps In The Road

In order to manage the bumps on the road, you need to get your mindset on surviving and healing so you don't stop dead in your tracks. With post-traumatic stress disorder (PTSD), you can have flashbacks, but you can recollect your thoughts, or *woosah* like I like to say, to calm yourself down. Then you can evaluate things.

The healed mind will now let you see it as a task to accomplish and not as a roadblock. You start thinking in a way that allows you to see a hurdle instead. Are you going to go up and over the hurdle, or are you going to go around to the left or around to the right? Now your open mind can see a way past it. There are always going to be roadblocks in your life, but now you can actually see the positives and know that you will still survive and come out the other side.

Trauma creates change you DON'T chose. Healing is about change you DO choose.

-Michelle Rosenthall

The most important part of how you handle it is your attitude. It is getting rid of the negative thoughts, tackling those roadblocks with positivity, and using it as a learning tool. It is critical not to instantly go back to the same mindset you had in the past, but use it as a steppingstone to go forward, evaluate it, dissect it, and choose the positive route.

It is about looking at roadblocks with a curious mind rather than with a judgmental one. Ask what is there to teach you. Road bumps happen to everybody. The real test of any individual is how resilient they are to setbacks. If you are reading this book, you have more resilience than you think. This is the time to use that skill to develop your resilience muscle.

Chapter Six

Step 3: Mental and Physical Health

The moment it hit me the worst was when I was in a relationship with a new person, and that person and the abuser held the same title of person in my life: my partner. When you come across the person who is in the same exact spot as the person that was the narcissist, it is super hard not to get defensive. It is hard to realise the person that is there now is not there to harm you. We all want to jump so quickly into a defensive mode and put up walls. It is also hard when you come across narcissists in other positions in your life, whether it is at work, at your parent's house, or wherever. You just have to stay focused and not let it be a setback.

When it is the exact same title of a person, it just makes it harder and can set you back a few steps. There is going to be some mental trauma. That is the number one thing you need to focus on healing. It is not easy seeing a kind, humble, supportive person and being able to trust them. There are going to be times when you question their motives, their truths, their intentions, or how they treat you.

Unless you take that step to heal that mental state, you are never going to move forward with a person that in the same chess piece. If you are the Queen and King, and you still think all Kings out there in the world are narcissists that treat you like that, you are never going to be able to heal.

For me, it was one unintentional comment my current husband made that made me feel unworthy and feel all of these things again. It wasn't his intention when he made the comment, but he didn't know how bad that comment would affect me. He was not being purposefully harmful; it was just the mental side of me that chose to pick out that tiny little spot in there and make it bigger than it really was. That will be one of your biggest roadblocks and you can't allow that to happen. It is not the same person. It is not the same issues. Those traumas tend to be really deep scars. Unless you use those scars as a steppingstone instead of a roadblock, you're never going to be able to move forward with anyone else in your life.

PTSD

I experienced PTSD every day. I never understood what PTSD or anxiety was. My ex would come home drunk or just looking for a fight, the door would slam, and my gut would sink. "Oh shit, he's home." I would tense up and wonder what would happen next.

Living in today's world, with happy-go-lucky people, where maybe my husband or daughter have their hands full, walk through the house and close the door a little too hard, the hair stands up on the back of your neck

Trauma is a fact of life. It does not, however, need to be a life sentence.

- Peter A. Levine

because you get an instant flashback. It makes you super tense and those are the things that you need to work on.

To come down off that tension and sickness that you feel inside, takes a lot longer than you could ever imagine. I remember one time I went to shoot guns in an indoor center. I actually love shooting guns and am not afraid of them, but when someone else uses them as a fear factor then it changes you. I went into the shooting center and before I could even get a shot off, I was shaking so bad and sick to my stomach. I just kept looking around at the other people in there and wondered what if they just turned on us and started shooting. I didn't know them. I didn't know how their mind works or what problems they have. What if they are like HIM? I just wanted to be removed from the situation. I was trying to not let my mind control the situation and I wanted to stay and have fun. I finally shot the gun a couple of times, but I couldn't take it anymore. I had so many things going through my head and flashbacks of incidents and times of fear. For me it felt like a claustrophobic reaction. I wanted to get out of there as soon as possible. I had to leave.

PTSD creates this overwhelming urge to look over your shoulder and watch your back. He used to threaten me with gun violence and told me on multiple occasions that one day he was going to pull the trigger and I would never see it coming. My anxiety can go through the roof whether it is when I stop at the mailbox to get my mail, when I come home and immediately scan the house because something seemed out of place, or the fact that I don't stand in front of the windows often just because in the back of my head he could pull the trigger from anywhere. In the back of my mind, I hear his voice telling me he could take me out anytime he wanted to and I wouldn't see it coming. Those repetitive remarks that were said year after year and engrained in your brain are one of the hardest things to get over, but you can get through it.

I didn't even realise I was doing those things until I travelled somewhere, like on my trip to Hawaii, and knew he really wasn't there. I was at peace. PTSD can be such a horrible thing as it can cause so many other health issues along the way. The heightened stress levels in your body triggers chemical responses in your body which can be harmful to your health in the short and long-term.

It is so important to face your fears and break down things in the moment that are a real danger, and those that aren't. A door slamming isn't a danger anymore, but stopping at the mailbox could be. What could I do to make myself more comfortable? Arm myself, learn protective measures to keep me and my family safe, which is smart to do regardless of dealing with a narcissist. For me, it was putting up security cameras, taking concealed carry classes, and just being more aware of things.

I could just hide in the house and wait for those noises to appear, but I am a problem solver. Never give up. Dissect it and you can always find a resolution and move forward. It may take time; the scars may be deep, but you can always crawl out of that hole. It just takes researching and finding what makes you feel comfortable. For me it never was a matter of being a victim and down on myself, it was a matter of survival and how I can get out, get things better and move on.

It didn't matter how she fell apart; it was how she put herself back together.

- Atticus

Remind yourself there are certain things to worry about, and certain things not to worry about. With the ones to worry about, find a resolution. I am worried about him sneaking into my house. Now I'm okay because there are cameras. You just need to find out what comforts you during those PTSD or anxiety moments. Then it is critical that you fact-check the things that stimulate you. In child psychology they call it detective thinking. You need to look at what's going on and ask, is that slamming door the same situation as when my husband came home in a rage? No, it's actually one of the teenaged children that was being too noisy so calm yourself and then continue on.

Fact-checking is useful, as is finding ways to give yourself comfort, whether that's physically by putting cameras up, or by finding people who understand what's going on that can help you or give you ideas.

Getting professional help is also valuable, because we can't tackle everything on our own. I tried to tackle it on my own for a very long time, and it wasn't until I saw the benefits my daughter had from professional help that I really understood. I used the same tools and furthered my healing process tremendously. I recommend looking outside the box and getting that professional help, even if it is hard to admit you need it.

You heal much faster with the benefit of an outside person looking in. It is like having a best friend that lets you complain about your job but corrects you when you need it. From the outside looking in someone reminds you that your job provides you with great joy and reminds you of things you love that about your job. Instead of letting you focus on the negative parts of your job. It gives you the ability to think on a broader range of things than you might be able to get to by yourself.

Professional help is there to empower you to develop new strategies, develop new skills, and see new solutions to the things holding you back. Professionals are also really good at pointing out areas where you're self-sabotaging, or where you are slowing down your healing progress you might not have noticed yet. It is an important step to get back to where you need to be.

Developing Resilience

Developing mental resilience is like a whole new world for me. I'm discovering a new person inside me I didn't know was there. I view things differently and in a more positive light than ever before in my life. The mental health journey gave me that. It is like learning something brand new. You get stuck in old ways. I felt like I had blinders on. I was in survival mode and didn't see anything outside of that. The mental health journey and healing process gave me a new light to help myself and others going through the same things.

I can bring out the joy they don't see, bring out the positivity they don't see. My husband and I call it bringing out the sunshine. I thrive in the sunshine. I'm smiling ear to ear. When you feel the warmth on you and you're just glowing, you can pass that on to others and help change lives. Try to be the light in someone's life and not the darkness. I love having the confidence and energy now to see one of my customers walk into my store and welcome them with a smile and an upbeat attitude and maybe just improve their day with a smile and a little caring. You never know what they are going through in their lives.

Autoimmune Diseases

Research shows that trauma can trigger auto immune diseases. Autoimmune diseases are debilitating and horrible. If I hadn't been through the mental healing, I feel I would still see autoimmune as a roadblock, but now I view it as a learning experience. I have learned more about my body and health on this journey than I ever have before. It gave me a sense of drive to find a resolution. It gave me goals.

To be honest, I don't want to say the autoimmune side of it was a positive by any means, but it gave me the will to climb to the to the top of the mountain and beat it, to prove I would not let the traumas of my past keep me down and not let this disease win. It also gave me more in-depth knowledge about my body, autoimmune diseases, health, wellness and a lot of good information to pass down to the next generation. To be honest, I knew nothing about health and wellness prior to and now I can not only help myself and my family, but I am helping people all over the country.

When I felt like I hit a brick wall and my health took a turn for the worst, it was traumatizing in itself. I had no energy, I had no strength, I was in horrible pain and I had my independence taken away once again. I was left at the mercy of others. I required my daughter to step up and do more chores, I required my husband to help me with tasks that I normally would handle myself, I had my step-daughter doing things like blow drying my hair because I couldn't hold my arms up to do it. It was humiliating, horrifying and then here came those PTSD moments also. You start fighting for your life all over again but in a different way. You try to have some dignity but thoughts of failure, thoughts of helplessness and thoughts of unworthiness take over. I knew I had lived through hell before and with a new mindset I was determined to tackle this with everything I had.

I survived because the fire inside of me burned brighter than the fire around me.

- Author Unknown

Chapter Seven

THE ROAD AHEAD

If you can't see the positive in this, let me tell you that this new health trauma led me into an entirely new business. I had a raging passion inside of me to not only help myself but to help others out there like me and help the next generations to come. When I was going through all of the testing and being tossed from doctor to doctor trying to figure out what was wrong, I felt helpless. I learned so much on my journey and so in depth, that I created my own health and wellness product. I am now releasing it out into the world to help people like me with PTSD, anxiety, and autoimmune.

Had I not been so debilitated by that autoimmune disease; I would never have filled my brain with the knowledge I have today. It is a little bit of freedom, self-sufficiency, and something that I have really enjoyed. I have been able to help people change their lives for the better and that is a life changing feeling in itself.

It is a positive thing and gives me a sense of knowing that I can be anything. There are setbacks with autoimmune, it tends to tear you down and you are extremely weak for days and weeks on end. It is really hard to get through, but there is a way to get through it and lesson the symptoms. You need to research and find out about your own body and what helps it.

Autoimmune diseases are where your body decides to attack itself. If you walk along and bump your knee on a table, to a normal person that would be a bruise, or it might hurt for a minute. To someone with autoimmune disease, all of your cells just rush to that area. That simple bump is now a completely swollen knee, your body is flooded with inflammation, and you feel like you're full of concrete. Now that is just an example that gives you a visual about it but on a normal basis it can feel like someone snuck in your house in the middle of the night with an IV of concrete and filled your body up and then wakes you up and says go do your daily tasks. When your body feels like that, it is really hard to do things and even more so, enjoy things.

It is horrifying, humiliating, and degrading. It is your body overdramatizing things and making the symptoms way worse than they need to be. To a strong minded, independent person, that is hard to take. The disease is destructive and deteriorates your joints and your health much faster than if you were healthy. It is an overreaction by your body's immune system to things that don't require that level or response.

It doesn't matter if it is an injury, or foods you eat your body doesn't know how to digest, your immune system floods in there and overreacts. It crashes, then over produces inflammation within your system which causes arthritic issues, pain, tiredness, and/or severe weakness. If a normal person ate some food they couldn't digest, they might feel a little sick to their stomach, an auto immune disease just takes it to the extreme. There is also an ungodly amount of pain associated with auto immune and that can wear on anyone's patience.

I researched every part of autoimmune diseases, did a lot of trial and error, excluded things from my life that didn't work, and also found the things that did work for me. I have an antioxidant and immune boosting juice that works really well for me. It gives my immune system the extra support it needs when it is weak and tired, and takes the inflammation out of my body so I don't feel like I have concrete in me. I didn't want to take prescriptions. When I did take them, I didn't feel like they were doing me good, just covering up some issues and causing some new ones.

I then discovered CBD. The benefits of CBD were extraordinary for me. I felt it was under mentioned for its anti-inflammatory abilities, anti-anxiety abilities and PTSD or at least it was still taboo and also not fully understood. We have an endocannabinoid system already in our bodies that CBD fits into like a hand to a glove. There are CB1 and CB2 receptors that we have that are found on the cell surfaces. CB! Receptors tie to the brain and central nervous system and the CB2 receptors tie to the immune system. These receptors play a key role in the bodies overall wellbeing. The research into CBD companies, the trial and error on products and finding out huge inconsistencies in the products on the market led me to developing my own. What does someone who has been through traumas and health issues want more than anything? To feel better and then to help others not go through the same.

I am no longer on any prescriptions, just this antioxidant and immune boosting juice and a CBD product that took me from operating at 20-30% to operating at 70-90%. It gives my immune system the fighting chance that it needs to operate on a better level.

Preventative Health

For people who have been through traumas, one area of preventative health at least to start focusing on is for anxiety. Whether you take a medicine or a natural approach like CBD, you want to stop it before it starts. If you feel an attack like a panic attack coming on, or if you have a lot of PTSD issues around slamming doors, loud noises, seeing him in a car driving, or other stressor points, you want to get ahead of that. If you let it go too far, it can bring down your health. You want to give your body the help that it needs.

For me, preventative is 100% the way to go because when I feel it coming on, it is basically my body reminding me to slow down. I boost my immune system, double up on my CBD, and work on keeping my energy up. If I don't have energy, I can't thrive, it feels like my body just doubles up on attacking me.
It is like trying to fight off the flu in cold season. When we start getting a runny nose, we all reach for a medicine, or in my case herbal stuff, or herbal teas to fight that off before it takes a full-blown effect. Heading it off is the key.

Developing resilience and learning to live with your physical and mental health is about being attuned to your body and jumping into the remedies that work for you, whatever they are. We may never be able to eradicate traumatic experiences and their effects on our life, but we can prevent the effects of them on our ongoing health. Get onto these early. Don't just let them go.
For example, if you are having an anxiety attack and jump on it quicker, it is more quickly resolved, but the

longer we let it go, the more pain and suffering we will go though.

Creating a Healthy Lifestyle For The Next Generation

Everything I've been through, and we are talking a long list of traumas and the health issues which are also traumas in themselves, has given me so much knowledge. I want to take that knowledge and pass it on to you and the next generation to known that no matter what you go through, you can survive. Not necessarily to make life so easy for everyone, but to give them the tools they need to use that knowledge to go forward. I want to see people thriving! I want to see my daughter and my step-children thriving! We can help them do that by giving them the knowledge and the tools to get through anything.

You're not a victim for sharing your story. You are a survivor setting the world on fire with your truth and you never know who needs your light, your warmth and raging courage.

- Alex Elle

I want to help change the next generations and help them have an easier journey instead of struggling for so many years and being stuck in concrete in the same spot. I want them to be able to walk through the concrete, get stuck there for a minute, then figure a way to keep going. I want them to know that you can always change your circumstances. You just need to arm yourself with knowledge and you can thrive, you just need to open your mind and keep going.

I am not one to do things FOR the kids because I feel like they won't learn as much. I want to help them. I want to educate them so that they have tools for the future. Arming our children with knowledge is the best thing that we can provide. Teach them never to give up. Teach them that no matter what life throws at them that they can dig deep, find a resolution, and still survive. There are so many things that life throws at us and my daughter has learned that first-hand also and it warms my heart to know that she wants to take what she has been through to then help others in life going through similar things.

If we all gave up when life would throw tough things at us, we would never learn anything. If I would have given up and just taken all of the medications that the doctors wanted me to take then I wouldn't have learned about the wonderful, natural CBD products that could help me with so many symptoms that I was having.

The Road Ahead

No matter how deep the scars are, no matter how big the hurdles and roadblocks are, or how many you are going to run across in your life, if you have a centered value of never giving up, things will always get better. You might not feel like it at a particular moment, but there is always a way out. There is always a way to change your life for the better. There is always a way to change your circumstances.

Your circumstances may be different to mine, and your pathway might be slightly different, but the elements are the same. First look at what is going on, get an assessment of where you are at and where you want to be. Then start to discover who you really are and what lights you up. Finally, deal with those physical and mental health issues. That is how you become that confident and secure person you were always meant to be.

Be the change you wish to see in the world

- Mahatma Ghandi

If you are working at a job you're not happy with, take the steps you need to go find one you are happy with. It is your choice to be stuck in concrete, or you can rise above it and thrive. If you are going through a lot of things like I did in my past, I'm here to tell you it will get better. I have had childhood abuse, lack of support system growing up, alcohol and drugs within the family, loss of my father, years and years of narcissist abuse, suicide awareness with my child, and my autoimmune disease that took my body down to almost immobile.

There is always another day, and in that day, you can change your circumstances. It might not be tomorrow, it might be a month down the road, it might be a year, but if you set goals and truly believe in yourself, want to live in positivity rather than negativity, then you can do anything you want.

Statistically, if you have been through childhood trauma, you are more likely to experience teen suicide, drug and alcohol problems, or prescription drug issues. The odds are stacked against you. It is the same with marriage problems. When we have problems and traumas like that, we have everything stacked against us saying we are damaged, we can't be fixed, or we are crazy.

Here I am with childhood traumas, marriage traumas, debilitating health issues, and I am still thriving. I did that because I never gave up on wanting to be a better person and wanting better health. I never gave up on wanting to heal my traumas, leave that stuff in the past, and be a better person and role model.

There are so many things that can stop us in our tracks, but if you never ever give up, life will get better. Let your scars teach you something and use that information to help you go from broken and afraid to confident and thriving!

One of my favorite songs is by Kelly Clarkson called Stronger. The message of that song is "what doesn't kill you makes you stronger" and I live with that every day as motivation and that is how I came up with using my scars as stepping stones and not as weights.

Chapter Eight

LET'S CONNECT

If you can't see the positive in this, let me tell you that my latest health trauma led me into an entirely new business. One I had a raging passion inside of me to do.

If you need motivation, inspiration and an energetic and driven person to help uplift you and get you on the track to thriving then reach out! I am here to show you that you CAN go from broken and afraid to confident and thriving. I can help you with the steps needed to heal your mind, let go of the trauma, and plan for a brighter future.

I believe everyone should know their worth and chase their dreams. I don't believe in settling, I think there is a big world out there and we should never limit ourselves to falling in line with other peoples idea of what a normal life should look like. I became an entrepreneur which takes drive, strength, and confidence. All of those qualities were something that I never thought I would have again. I have beaten all the odds stacked against me and am living proof of how we have the opportunity to change our circumstances with every new day. No matter what has been thrown my way from childhood to adulthood, I never gave up and have risen every time I was knocked down.

What will your new life and journey look like? What does the confident you look like? What will you accomplish? What will you pass down to the next generations?

You can connect with me by joining my Unbreakable, Unstoppable & Driven ~Livin' A Happy Life Facebook group at the link below.

https://www.facebook.com/groups/unbreakableunstoppable/?ref=share

You can also reach out to me at
WWW. AngelaNewhouse.Com.

I want to help as many people deal with your own situation as I can. Below are some worksheets and resources that I use with my clients. Please download and share them widely.

https://angelanewhouse.com/landing/reveal-my-path
https:angelanewhouse.com/members/vaults/2551

Learn more at
https://angelanewhouse.com

www.ingramcontent.com/pod-product-compliance
Lightning Source LLC
Chambersburg PA
CBHW021955290426
44108CB00012B/1082